Word 2000 Intermediate

Chris Voyse and Patrice Muse

Published by
Voyse Recognition Limited

October 2006

© 2006 Voyse Recognition Limited

This guide has been designed in order to create a methodical approach to learning this product. Our website www.smart-pc-guides.com outlines all the guides in the Office 2003 portfolio that © Voyse Recognition Limited produce.

All rights reserved. No part of this publication may be reproduced stored in a retrieval system, mechanical, photocopy, recording or otherwise without prior consent of the publisher. All trademarks used herein are the property of their respective owners. The use of any trademark in this text does not vest in the author or publisher any trademark ownership rights in such trademarks, nor does the use of such trademarks apply any affiliation with or endorsement of the guides by such owners.

Notice of Liability

Every effort has been made to ensure that these guides contain accurate and current information. However, © Voyse Recognition Limited or any associated company shall not be liable for any loss or damage suffered by readers as a result of any information contained herein.

First Published in Great Britain in 2006

Voyse Recognition Limited
Century Business Centre
Manvers Way
Manvers
Rotherham
South Yorkshire
S63 5DA
01709 300188

ISBN 1-905657-15-3

ISBN 978-1-905657-15-5

Intermediate Level Objectives

- Working with Tables
- Section and Page Breaks
- Setting Tabs
- Working with Styles
- Creating New Styles
- Define and Locate Bookmarks
- Generate a Table of Contents
- Creating an Index
- The AutoSummarise Feature
- Reviewing a Document using Track Changes
- Using Comments
- Creating a Mail Merge
- Using Mail Merge to Create Labels
- Templates

Table of Contents

Intermediate Level Objectives 3
Working with Tables 6
   Using the AutoFit Feature 6
   The AutoFormat Feature 6
   To Delete a Table Style 9
   Using the Table and Borders Toolbar 10
Exercise 1: - Creating a Booking Form 11
Different Types of Breaks 12
   To Create a Section Break 12
   To Delete a Page, Column or Section Break 13
Changing Header and Footer Information 13
   Moving between Sections of a Document 14
Exercise 2: - Creating a Header and Footer 15
Identify the Tab Stop Marker 16
   Different Tab and Indent Icons 16
Exercise 3: - Creating Tabs in a Document 18
What are Styles? 19
   How to View Styles in a Document 19
   Working with Styles using the Formatting Toolbar 20
   Using the Styles and Formatting Area 20
   To Modify a Style 21
   Adding a Style to a Template 22
   The Automatically Update Feature 22
   Creating a New Style 23
   Assigning a Shortcut Key to a New Style 24
   Deleting a Style already added to a Template 25
Exercise 4: - Creating a Document Using Styles 28
Bookmarks 29
   To Add a Bookmark 29
   To Locate a Bookmark 29
   To Delete a Bookmark 30
Creating a Table of Contents 30
Moving within a Table of Contents 31
Exercise 5: - Update a Table of Contents 32
Indexes 33
   Creating an Index using the Menu Bar 33
AutoSummarise 36
   To Read a Summary of an Online Document 36
   To Alter the Display of a Document 37
   Display or Highlight Key Points in a Document 37
   To Create a Summary or Abstract 38
Reviewing a Document using Track Changes 38
   How to use Track Changes 38
Using Comments 38
   To Insert a Comment 38
   To Edit a Comment 38
   To Delete a Comment 39

Using the Review Pane 39
Accept all Changes made to a Document 39
    Compare Two Copies of a Document... 39
Mail Merge... 40
    Creating Letters using Mail Merge 40
    Creating Labels using Mail Merge 49
Exercise 6: - Creating Labels 56
Templates.. 57
    To Save a Document as a Template 57
    Open and Amend an Existing Template 58
Notes Page.. 59
Expert Level Objectives... 60

Working with Tables

Using the AutoFit Feature

AutoFit automatically resizes rows and columns to the size of their contents.

1. Click anywhere inside the table
2. Select T**a**ble, **A**utoFit, select Auto**F**it to Contents

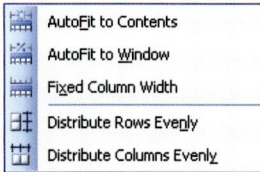

Figure 1

3. The cells are automatically adjusted to fit their contents

The AutoFormat Feature

Use the AutoFormat feature to quickly customise a table to suit individual needs.

1. Select the table to format, choose T**a**ble,

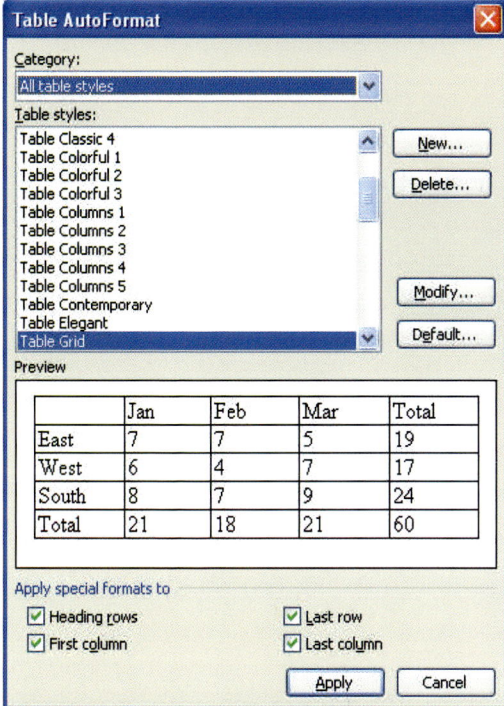

Figure 2

2. Select a format style in **T**able Styles
3. The Preview area displays the selected style
4. Select [New...], the Modify Style dialog appears

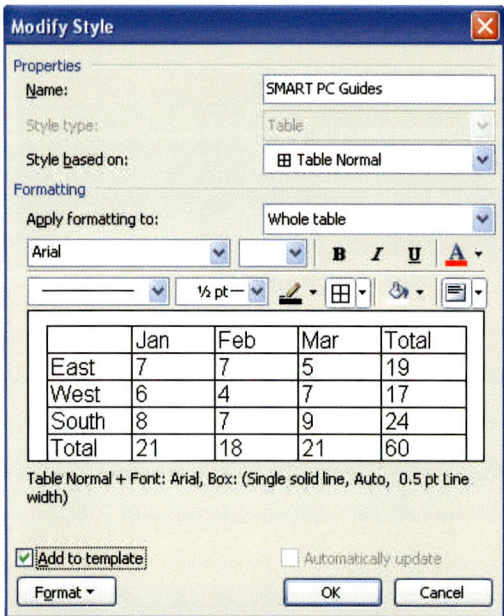

Figure 3

5. Choose **N**ame, type SMART PC Guides

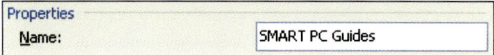

Figure 4

6. Change the Font style to Arial
7. Format the table as required, click in the **A**dd to template box
8. Click `OK`, press `Apply`

To Delete a Table Style

1. Choose T<u>a</u>ble, [Table Auto<u>F</u>ormat...]

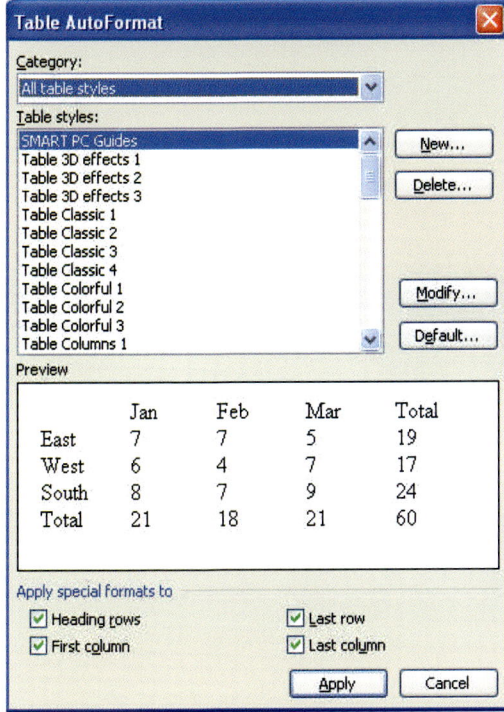

Figure 5

2. In the <u>T</u>able styles dialog box, select SMART PC Guides
3. Press [Delete...], the following prompt appears

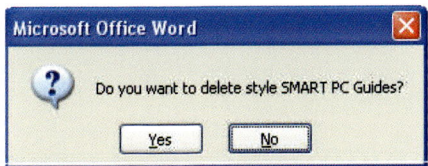

Figure 6

4. Click [Yes], select [Close]

Using the Table and Borders Toolbar

1. Select a table
2. Click on the Table and Borders icon
3. Or select <u>V</u>iew, <u>T</u>oolbars, Tables and Borders

Figure 7

4. To design, draw and create a table click on the Draw Table icon
5. In the status bar the following prompt appears

Click and drag to create table and to draw rows, columns and borders.

Figure 8

6. Drag using the left button to create a table by drawing rows and columns
7. To deselect click on the Draw Table icon
8. To rotate text, select the text to be rotated
9. Click on the Change Text Direction icon
10. To merge cells, highlight the cells to be merged, click on Merge Cells icon
11. The Split Cells icon divides cells into smaller rows or columns
12. Click in a cell, choose the Split Cells icon
13. The Split Cells dialog box appears

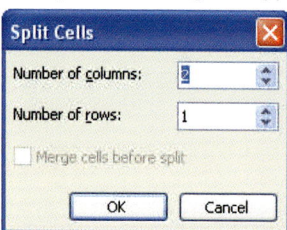

Figure 9

14. Enter the number of columns or rows, click OK
15. The Eraser icon enables lines to be deleted from the table
16. Press the Eraser icon, click on the line with the left button
17. To sort items alphabetically/numerically select Sort Ascending icon
18. The Sort Descend icon sorts items in a descending order

Exercise 1: - Creating a Booking Form

SMART PC Guides Travel Services			
Departure Information			
Reservation Reference:		Destination	
UK Departure Airport		Name of Airport	
Date of Travel			
Number of Nights			

Title	Initial	Surname (in Capitals)		Insurance	
				Yes	
				Yes	Delete YES if you have arranged alternative insurance which is valid for your travel dates
				Yes	
				Yes	
				Yes	
				Yes	NAME OF INSURER:
				Yes	
				Yes	
				Yes	
				Yes	

Arrival Date	Hotel Name	Resort	No of Nights

Full Address and Telephone Number of First Named Adult		
		Telephone Number
Signed		Date

1. Create the above Booking Form Using Tables
2. Save it as SMART PC Guides Travel Services Booking Form.doc

Different Types of Breaks

The following information will be visible when using breaks in Normal View.

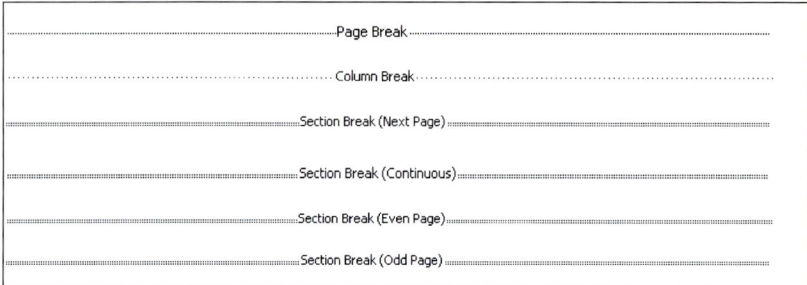

Figure 10

To Create a Section Break

1. Click Normal View
2. Select the place in a document where a section break is required
3. Select **I**nsert, **B**reak, the Break dialog box appears

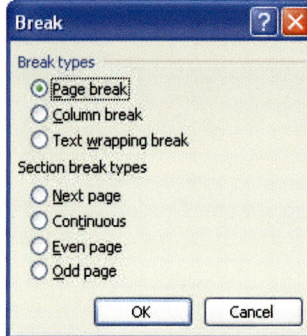

Figure 11

4. Select **N**ext page, click OK
5. Choose **F**ile, Page Set**u**p, Orientation, Land**s**cape
6. Select This section in the Appl**y** to box

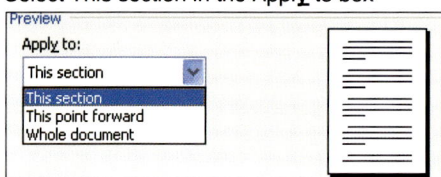

Figure 12

7. Click [OK]
8. Print Preview displays the new section in landscape, close Print Preview
9. Create a new Section Break follow steps 2 to 6, change to Portrait
10. Print Preview displays 2 pages in portrait and one in landscape
11. Close Print Preview, return to Page 1 in the document
12. Select View, Header and Footer
13. Section 1 is displayed above the header box Header -Section 1-
14. Type Section 1 inside the header box, select the Show Next icon
15. Choose Link to Previous Section icon
16. Type Section 2 inside the header box, click on Show Next icon
17. Select Link to Previous icon
18. Type Section 3 inside the header box
19. Click on Switch between Header and Footer icon
20. Select [Insert AutoText ▼], choose Page X of Y, press [Close]
21. Save the document as Working with Sections.doc, preview the results

To Delete a Page, Column or Section Break

1. Select Normal View, click the left button on the break you want to delete
2. Press the delete key to remove the break from the document

Changing Header and Footer Information

Header and Footer Toolbar Options	
Icon	Descriptive Prompt
Insert AutoText ▼	Displays pre set options
	Inserts the Page Number
	Inserts Number of Pages
	Format Page Number
	Insert Date
	Insert Time
	Page Setup
	Show/Hide Document Text
	Link to Previous
	Switch Between Header and Footer
	Show Previous
	Show Next
Close	Close

Figure 13

Moving between Sections of a Document

1. Select <u>V</u>iew, <u>H</u>eader and Footer to display the cursor in the Header area

Figure 14

2. Choose the Show Next icon to take you to the next section
3. Click on the Show Previous icon to go back to the previous section
4. Select the switch between the Header and Footer icon
5. The Show Next and Show Previous icons take you to the next or previous sections of the Footer
6. Choose Close

Note: To view information in a Header or Footer area select the Print Layout View

Exercise 2: - Creating a Header and Footer

1. Open SMART PC Guides Travel Services Booking Form.doc
2. Centre align and type SMART PC Guides Booking Form in the Header
3. Go to the Footer and insert Page 1 of 1
4. Save the document

Identify the Tab Stop Marker

Setting tabs allows you to quickly create and align information in a document.

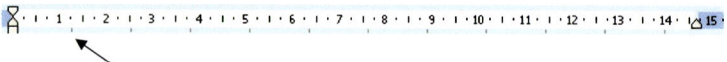

The default tab marker is set at 1.27cm

Figure 15

1. Select a new blank document
2. Click on the Show/Hide ¶ icon with the left button
3. Press Tab to move to the next default tab marker below the ruler
4. A tab stop is identified by a vertical grey line
5. The default tab is left aligned the text appears from the left

Different Tab and Indent Icons

The following tab icons are displayed on the left hand side of the ruler

Icons	Description of Icons in the Ruler
L	Left Tab
⊥	Centre Tab
⌐	Right Align Tab
⊥	Decimal Tab
׀	Bar Tab
▽	First Line Indent
⊔	Hanging Indent

Figure 16

Setting Tabs from the Ruler
1. Move the mouse pointer over the left align L icon
2. Click with the left button, (the icon changes with each click)
3. Click with you left button to display the different tab options
4. Choose the left alignment tab L
5. Move the mouse pointer to 3cm on the ruler
6. Click with the left button, the Left tab is set
7. Set a Right tab at 13 cm and a Decimal tab at 7.5cm
8. Insert a Bar tab at 5cm and 10cm
9. The set tabs are shown below

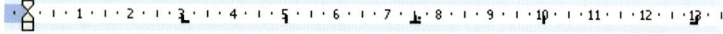

Figure 17

Remove Tabs from the Ruler

1. Move the mouse pointer over the left align icon in the ruler
2. Click and hold down the left button
3. Drag the selected tab off the ruler, the tab is removed from the ruler

Setting Tabs using the Menu Bar

1. Select F**o**rmat, **T**abs from the Menu Bar

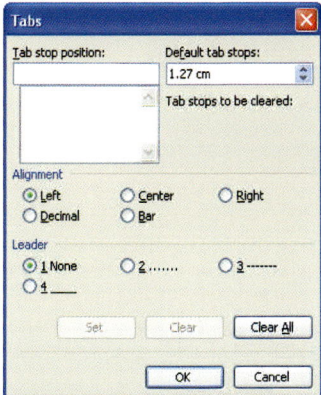

Figure 18

2. Select the **T**ab stop position
3. Type 3cm as the measurement for the tab stop
4. Select the Alignment **L**eft, click Set
5. Repeat the above steps to set additional alignments
6. To remove an alignment click on the measurement
7. Click Clear, select OK
8. Selecting Clear All reverts back to the default tab

Exercise 3: - Creating Tabs in a Document

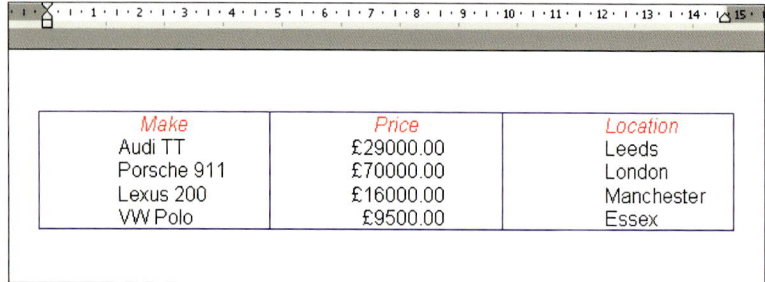

1. Select a new blank document
2. Create a table with 3 columns and 1 row
3. Set a centre tab in column 1 at 2.5cm
4. Use the Format Painter to copy the format to column 2 and 3
5. Or use [Tab] to move to the next column
6. Use [Ctrl] and [Tab] to move to the set tab within the column
7. Type the headings in each column
8. Press [Enter] to create a new line in the table
9. Click with the left button after the heading named **Make**, select [Enter]
10. Create the new tab stop for the remaining text
11. Set a left tab in column 1 at 1.5cm
12. Set a decimal tab in column 2 at 3cm
13. Set a left tab in column 3 at 2cm
14. Type in the text
15. Save the Document as Working with Tabs.doc

What are Styles?

A style is a series of formats that can be applied to individual characters or entire paragraphs that enhance the appearance of documents. A table of contents can be created using the styles formatted in the document.

Styles enable you to change the format of documents, for example changing font, colour and typeface, alter alignments, indenting and line spacing, add number and bullet lists and create style headings and sub-headings. If styles are used in a document a Table of Contents can be generated automatically based upon the styles that have been formatted.

How to View Styles in a Document

1. Select Normal View 🔲 or Outline View 🔲
2. Select **T**ools, **O**ptions, View

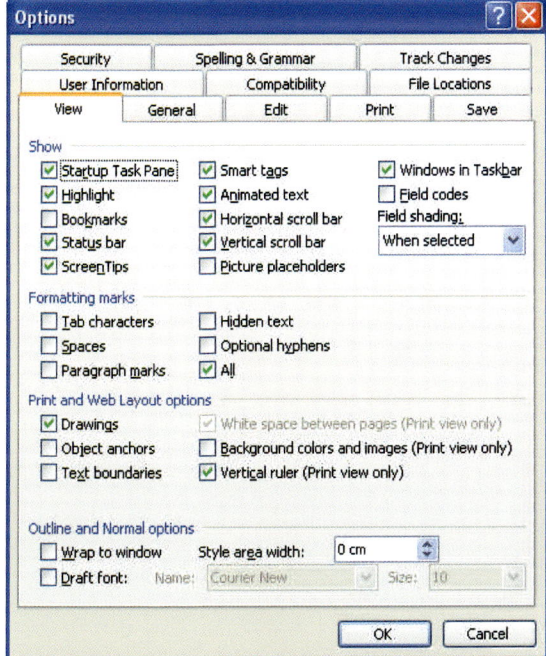

Figure 19

3. Select Style ar**e**a width, change the measurement to 2cm

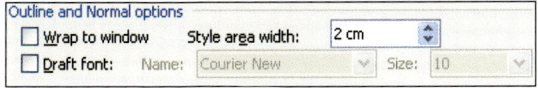

Figure 20

4. Select 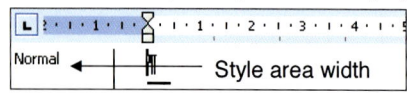, the Style area is displayed in the document

Figure 21

Working with Styles using the Formatting Toolbar

1. Select Format, Styles and Formatting…
2. Alternatively, click on the Styles area in the Formatting toolbar

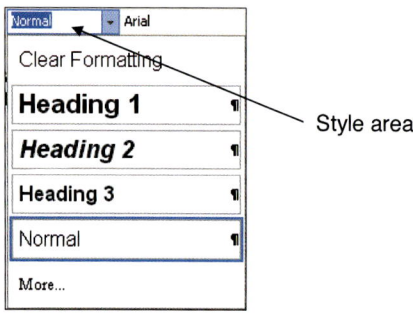

Figure 22

3. Select Heading 1, type SMART PC Guides Limited
4. Select Heading 2, 3 and Normal Style to view the different styles

Using the Styles and Formatting Area

1. Click on a new blank document
2. Select F**o**rmat, Styles and Formatting…
3. The dialog box appears on the right hand side of the screen

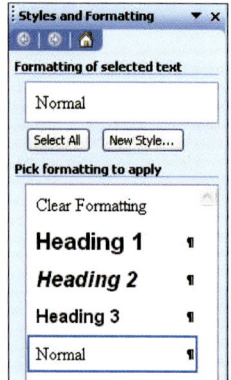

Figure 23

4. Choose Heading 1

5. Follow the steps in the previous section Working with Styles
6. To clear formatting click on `Clears formatting and styles from selected text`

`Clear Formatting`

Figure 24

To Modify a Style

1. Open a new blank document
2. Select F**o**rmat, `Styles and Formatting...`
3. Choose Heading 1, click with the right button, select **M**odify

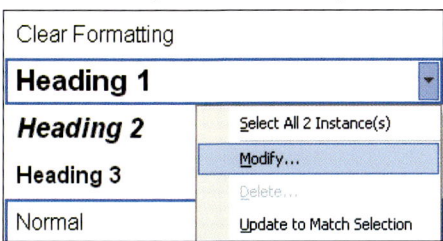

Figure 25

4. The Modify Style dialog box appears

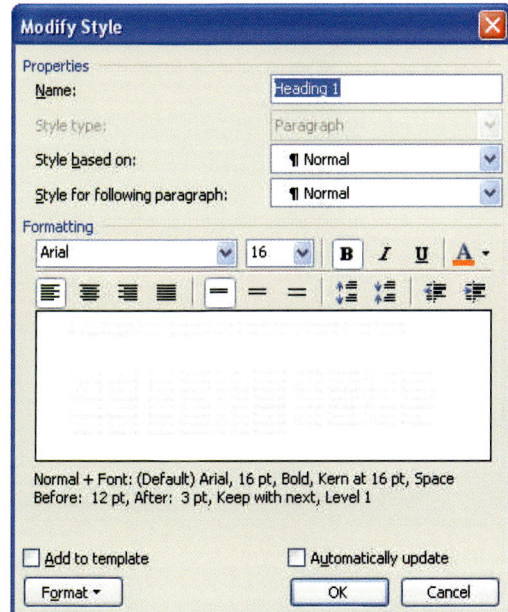

Figure 26

5. Change the formatting options as required, select [Format ▼]

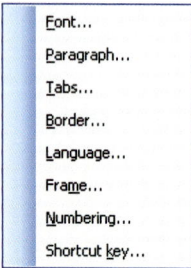

Figure 27

6. Click Font, change the colour, choose [OK]
7. **Do not select** the Add to template option or Automatically Update option
8. Click [OK]
9. The modified style appears in the [Styles and Formatting ▼] task pane

Adding a Style to a Template

To add a style to a template, tick [☑ Add to template] in the Modify Style dialog box.

The Automatically Update Feature

Use the automatic update feature with extreme care. Any changes made to the alignment of a document using the [☐ Automatically update] option changes all the text.

Creating a New Style

1. Click on a new blank document
2. Select F**o**rmat, [Styles and Formatting...], choose [New Style...]

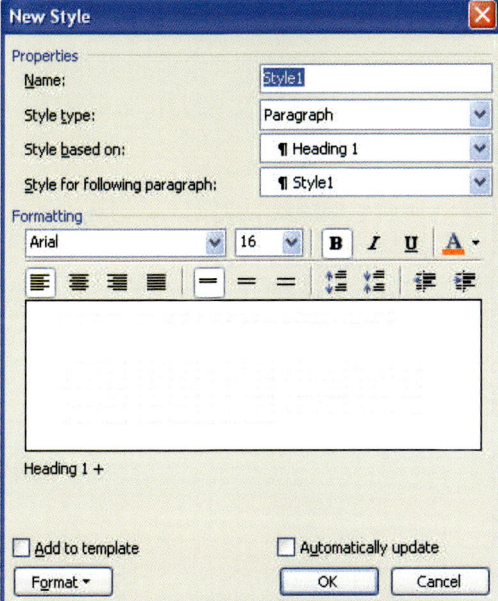

Figure 28

3. Select **N**ame, type [SMART PC Guides New Style]
4. Click [Format ▼], modify the style to your requirements
5. Click [OK] the New Style dialog box appears
6. Select [OK] to return to the document
7. The style appears in the [Styles and Formatting ▼] area and is ready to use

Assigning a Shortcut Key to a New Style

1. Choose SMART PC Guides New Style
2. Click with the right button, select **Modify...**

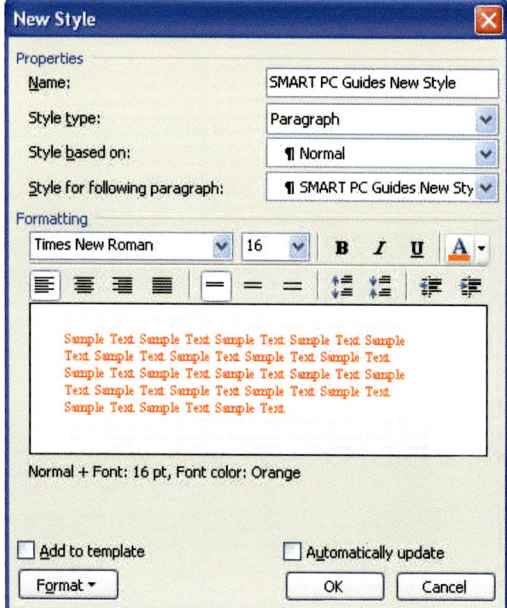

Figure 29

3. Click with the left mouse button on F**o**rmat
4. Select **Shortcut key...**, the Customise Keyboard dialog box appears
5. SMART PC Guides New Style appears in the **Commands:** box
6. Go to **Press new shortcut key:**
7. Hold down the **Alt** key, press **5**
8. Click **Assign**, choose **Close**
9. Click with the left button in the **☐ Add to template** dialog box
10. Select **OK**

Deleting a Style already added to a Template

1. Click F**o**rmat,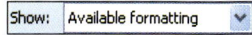
2. If the style to be deleted cannot be seen select

   Show: Available formatting

   Figure 30
3. Select SMART PC Guides New Style
4. Click on the downward arrow after available formatting
5. In the Show area select Custom...

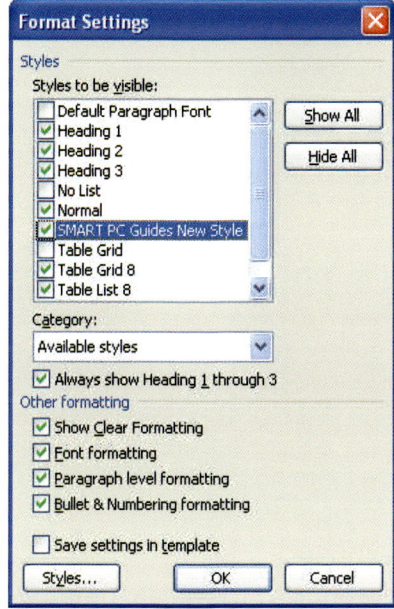

Figure 31

6. Select SMART PC Guides New Style, select Styles...

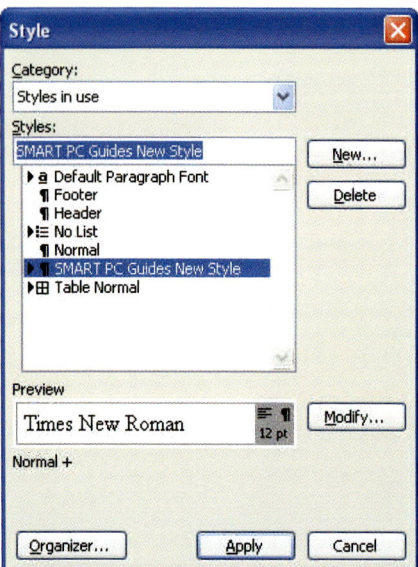

Figure 32

7. To delete the style from the template select [Organizer...]

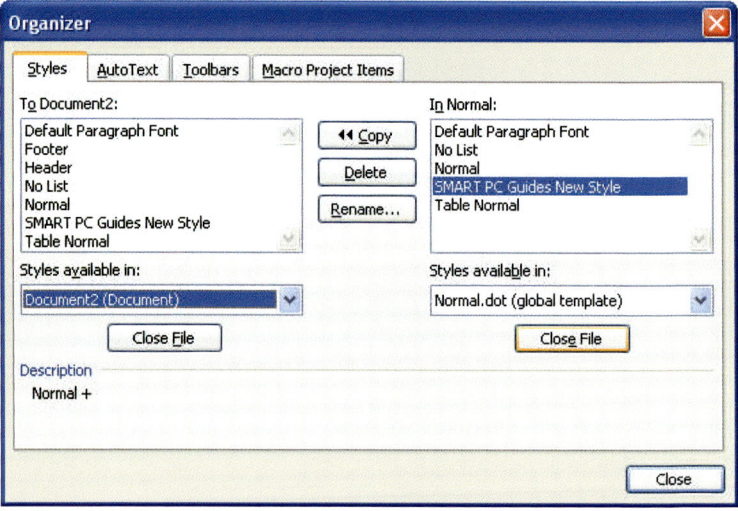

Figure 33

8. Go to I**n** Normal box, select SMART PC Guides New Style, click [Delete]

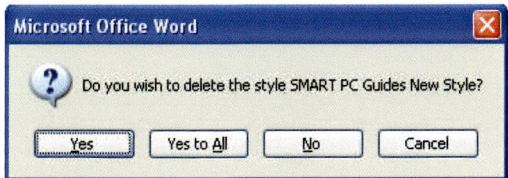

Figure 34

9. Choose [Yes to All]
10. The style is deleted from the Normal.dot template
11. Click [Close]

Exercise 4: - Creating a Document Using Styles

1. Open a new blank document
2. On Page 1 select Heading Style 1, type Monday
3. Press [Enter], select Heading Style 2, type Briefing at 10.00
4. On Page 2 select Heading Style 1, type Tuesday
5. Press [Enter], select Heading Style 2, type Performance Review at 15.00
6. On Page 3 select Heading Style 1, type Wednesday
7. Press [Enter], select Heading Style 3, type Progress Meeting 09.30
8. On Page 4 select Heading Style 1, type Thursday
9. Press [Enter], select Heading Style 2, type Staff Appraisal at 14.15
10. On Page 5 select Heading Style 1, type Friday
11. Press [Enter], select Heading Style 3, type Company Car New Criteria
12. Preview the document, check the newly created styles on each page
13. Save the document as Working with Styles
14. Close the document

Bookmarks

By setting a bookmark, text can be found easily for future reference.

To Add a Bookmark

1. Click with the left button where you want to add a bookmark
2. Select Insert, Bookmark and type the bookmark name

Figure 35

3. Click Add

Note: The underscore character can be used to separate words.

To Locate a Bookmark

1. Click Insert, Bookmark, select the bookmark name

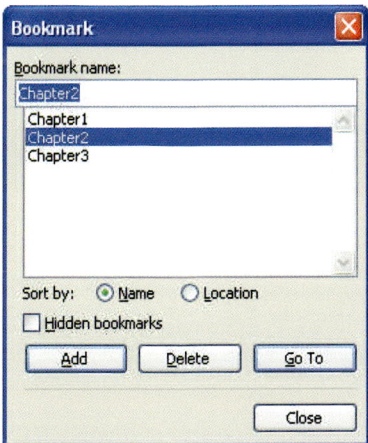

Figure 36

2. Click [Go To], choose [Close]

To Delete a Bookmark

1. Select Insert, Bookmark
2. Select the name of the bookmark you want to delete
3. Click [Delete], press [Close]

Creating a Table of Contents

A Table of Contents is a structured list of a document's content. If the document was constructed using styles, a Table of Contents can be generated automatically.

1. Open the document Working with Styles
2. Hold down the [Ctrl] and Home keys, go to page 1
3. Select Normal View, create a page break
4. Click in the new page, press [Enter]
5. Ensure the cursor is at the top of the new page
6. Choose Normal Style using the Formatting toolbar
7. Change the font to Arial, size 14, Bold
8. Centre align and type out Table of Contents on the first page
9. Press [Enter], Select, Align Left
10. Select Insert, [Reference] ▶ [Index and Tables...]

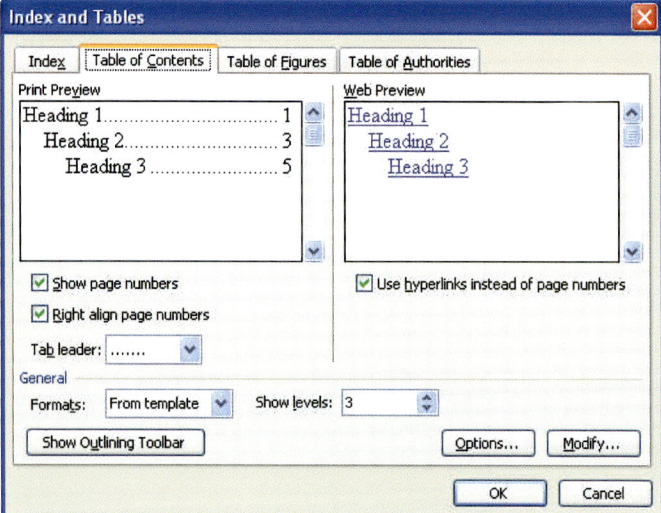

Figure 37

11. Select the Table of **C**ontents tab
12. Print Pre**v**iew displays the layout of the Table of Contents
13. Select
14. Select [OK] the Table of Contents appears in the document

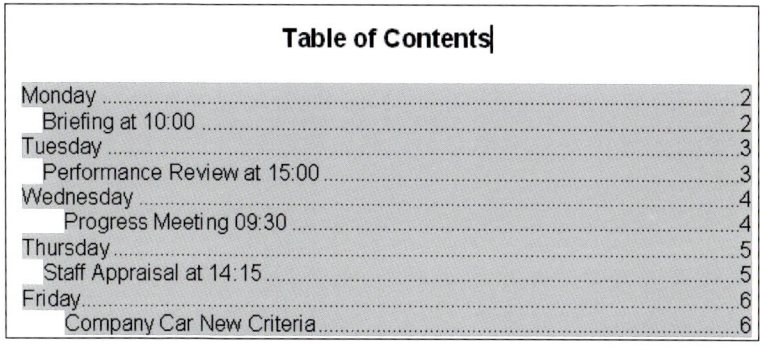

Figure 38

15. Save the document

Figure 39

Moving within a Table of Contents

1. To go to page 3 in the Table of Contents
2. Hold down [Ctrl], move the mouse pointer over page 3
3. The mouse pointer changes to
4. Click on the page number, page 3 appears
5. Save and close the document

Exercise 5: - Update a Table of Contents

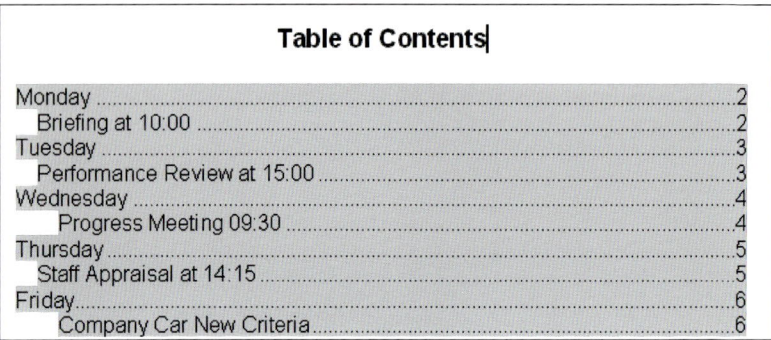

1. Open the document Working with Styles
2. Select **V**iew, **T**oolbars, Outlining

3. Hold down [Ctrl], move the mouse pointer over page 2
4. Click on the page number, the cursor appears on page 2
5. Change Briefing at 10:00 to Heading Style 3, click [Update TOC]
6. Select Update **e**ntire table

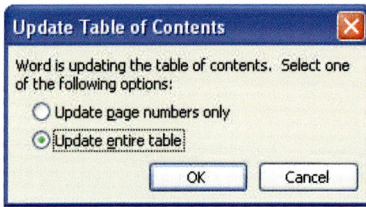

7. Choose [OK]
8. Change Company Car New Criteria to Heading Style 2, click [Update TOC]
9. Update the entire table
10. Click Go to TOC icon to view the updated Table of Contents
11. Save the document

Indexes

Long documents normally have a reference guide at the back of the document known as an index. The index identifies keywords and subjects frequently used in a document.

Creating an Index using the Menu Bar

1. Open the document Working with Styles
2. Select **I**nsert, Refere**n**ce, In**d**ex and Tables
3. Choose Inde**x** tab

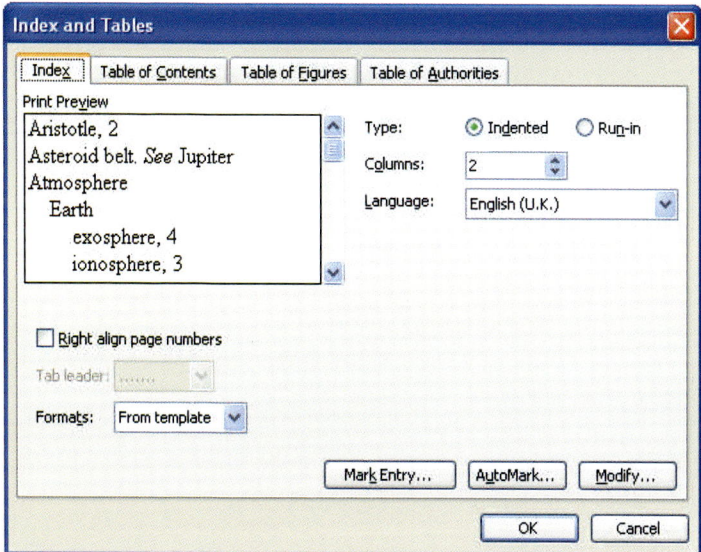

Figure 40

4. Select [Type: Indented], choose [Columns: 1]
5. Change the dialog as below

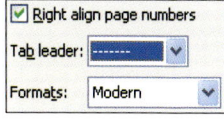

Figure 41

6. Click [Mar**k** Entry...]

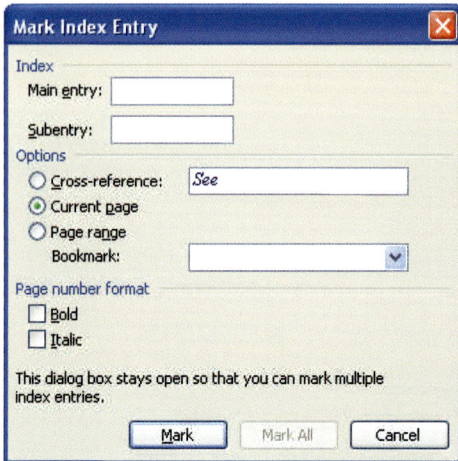

Figure 42

7. Create Main **e**ntries and **S**ubentries from the table below

Select	In Mark Index Type	Click
Main **e**ntry	Monday	Mark
Subentry	Briefing	Mark
Main **e**ntry	Briefing	Mark
Subentry	Monday	Mark
Main **e**ntry	Tuesday	Mark
Subentry	Performance	Mark
Main **e**ntry	Performance	Mark
Subentry	Review	Mark
Main **e**ntry	Review	Mark
Subentry	Tuesday	Mark

Figure 43

8. Create Main **e**ntry and **S**ubentries for Wednesday to Friday
9. Click `Close`
10. Go to the end of the document and create a new page
11. Select **I**nsert, `Reference` ▶ `Index and Tables...`
12. Click `OK`
13. The finished Index is illustrated on the next page

A

Appraisal
  Thursday --------5

B

Briefing
  Monday --------2

C

Company Car
  Friday --------6

F

Friday
  Company Car --------6

M

Monday
  Briefing --------2

P

Performance
  Review --------3
  Tuesday --------3
Progress
  Wednesday --------4

R

Review
  Performance --------3

T

Thursday
  Appraisal --------5
Tuesday
  Performance --------3

W

Wednesday
  Progress --------4

Figure 44

AutoSummarise

The AutoSummarise feature gives a score to each sentence based on the number of words most frequently used in a sentence. Word automatically summarises these key points to create a summary for others to read. You can then select how much detail you wish to use in the summary.

To Read a Summary of an Online Document

1. Open or type the document that requires a summary
2. Select <u>V</u>iew, <u>P</u>rint Layout View
3. Select <u>T</u>ools, A<u>u</u>toSummarize…
4. The AutoSummarise helper appears

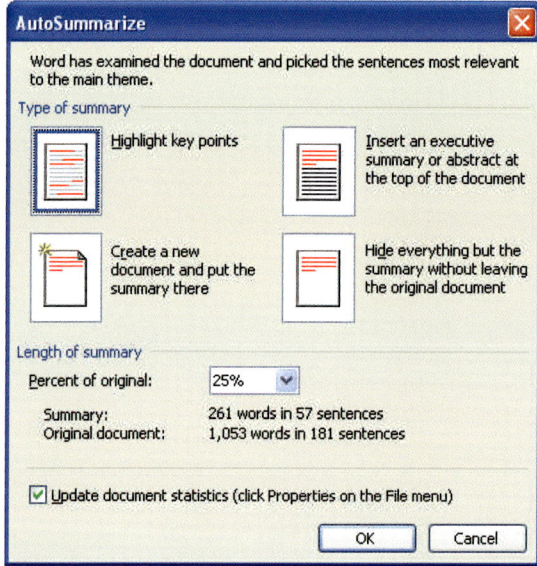

Figure 45

5. Select Type of summary
6. Click in the box to select the way you want to view the document
7. Select Percent of original: 25%
8. Use the arrow keys to select how much detail is required
9. Click OK
10. The summary appears at the beginning of the document

To Alter the Display of a Document

1. Open or type the document that requires a summary
2. Select View, Print Layout View, choose Tools, AutoSummarise
3. Select Type of summary

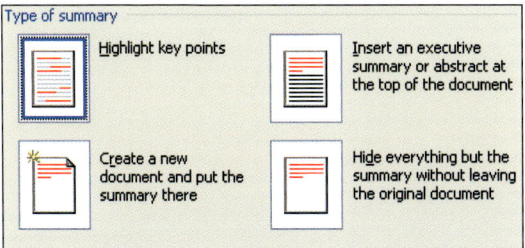

Figure 46

4. Click the Highlight key points box, press OK
5. The AutoSummarise toolbar appears

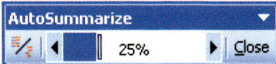

Figure 47

Display or Highlight Key Points in a Document

1. Click on the Highlight/Show Only summary icon

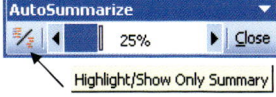

Figure 48

2. To adjust the level of detail drag the blue slider with the left button
3. Alternatively, click the arrows in the AutoSummarise toolbar
4. To increase or decrease the content of the summary, click in the AutoSummarise toolbar
5. Hold down the Shift key, rotate the wheel on the mouse
6. This increases or decreases the detail in the summary in 5% increments
7. Click Close

To Create a Summary or Abstract

1. Select <u>T</u>ools, A<u>u</u>toSummarise
2. Select Type of summary, choose how the summary is to be displayed
3. Select the level of detail to be included in the summary
4. Select the Percentage of original box, click [OK]
5. To delete a summary, click the Undo [↺] icon or modify the summary manually

Note: AutoSummarise automatically searches documents for keywords and sentences that represent discussed topics; it then copies these to Keywords and Comments boxes. To view Keywords and Comments, select File, Properties, Summary.

Reviewing a Document using Track Changes

Track Changes allows you to make and view changes and comments made to a document.

How to use Track Changes

1. Select <u>V</u>iew, <u>T</u>oolbars, Reviewing

Figure 49

2. Click on the Track Changes [icon] icon
3. Highlight the text in the document that requires a change
4. Press Delete
5. The deleted text is displayed on the right-hand side of the document
6. New text inserted is highlighted and underlined

Using Comments

To Insert a Comment

1. Click where the comment is to appear, select the Insert Comment [icon] icon
2. Type in the required text for the comment
3. The comment is displayed on the right-hand side of the document

To Edit a Comment

1. Select the comment to be edited
2. Click in the comment box on the right-hand side of the document
3. Edit the comment as required

To Delete a Comment

1. Select the comment to be deleted
2. Click in the comment box on the right hand side of the document
3. Select Reject Change/Delete Comment icon

Using the Review Pane

1. Select the Reviewing Pane icon
2. The changes and comments pane appears at the bottom of the screen
3. Use the arrow keys to scroll up and down the pane
4. Click on the Reviewing Pane icon to return to the original document

Accept all Changes made to a Document

1. Open an existing document
2. Select the Previous or Next icons to view changes
3. Review the changes made in the document
4. To accept changes click on the Accept Changes icon
5. To reject change or delete a comment
6. Choose the Reject Change/Delete icon

Compare Two Copies of a Document

1. Open the original document, select **T**ools, Compare and Merge **D**ocuments

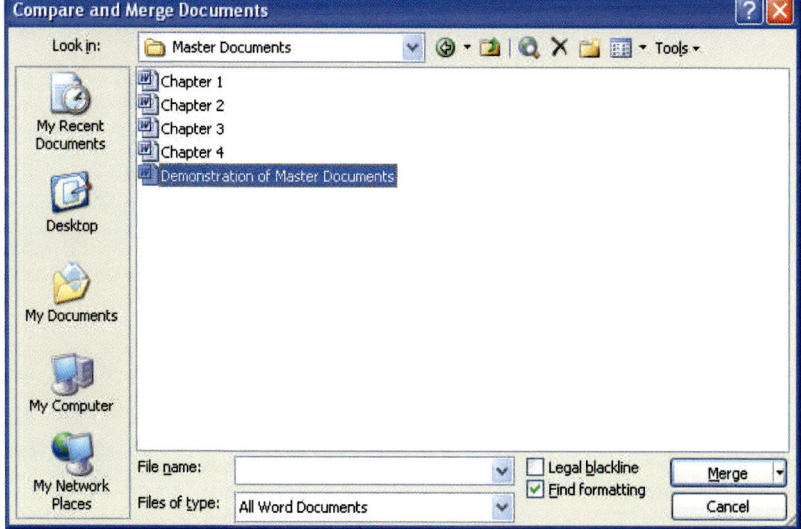

Figure 50

2. Locate the edited document, click once to highlight the document
3. To accept the changes, select Merge into **c**urrent document

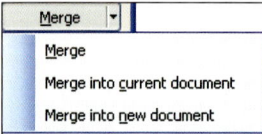

Figure 51

Mail Merge

Mail Merge is a quick way of merging information from one document into another allowing you to send personalised letters to groups of people or individuals by creating a main letter and a list of addresses that Word merges automatically. In order to do this two documents are needed, a Main document and a Data document.

Creating Letters using Mail Merge

1. Select open new document
2. Click on **T**ools, L**e**tters and Mailings, **M**ail Merge

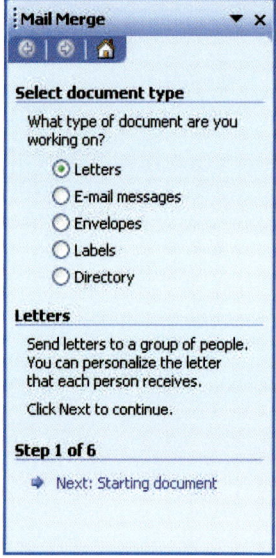

Figure 52

3. Select Letters from the document type
4. Click on Next: Starting Document to move to Step 2

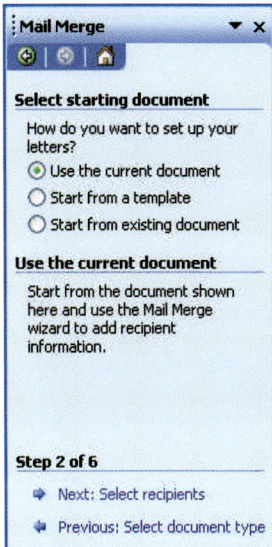

Figure 53

5. Select Use the current document
6. Click on Next: Select recipients to move to Step 3

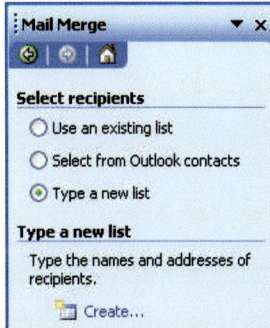

Figure 54

7. Choose Type a new list, click Create
8. The New Address List dialog box appears

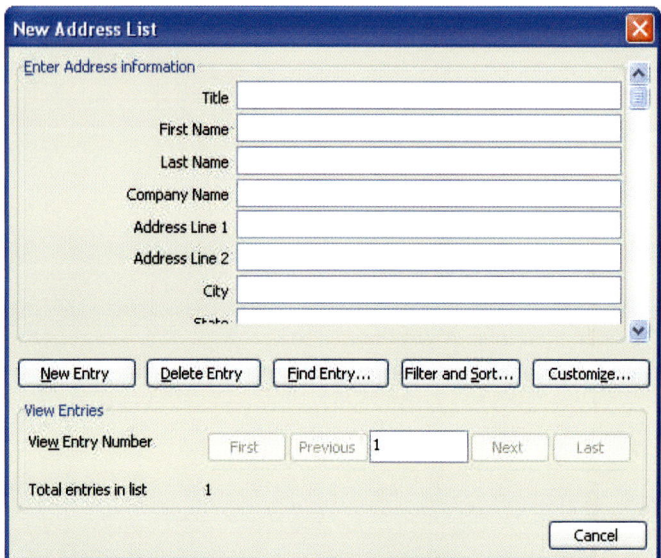

Figure 55

9. Select [Customize...]

Figure 56

10. Edit Field Names as required

11. Select State, press [Rename]

Figure 57

12. Type County, click [OK]
13. Edit the Customise List as below

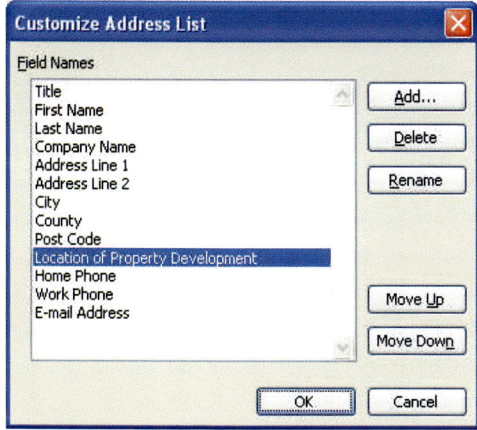

Figure 58

14. Add the following **F**ield Names: Venue Location and Date of Seminar
15. Click [OK] to return to the New Address List
16. Enter the Address List as below

First Name	Last Name	Company Name	Address Line 1	Address Line 2	City	Home Phone	Work Phone	Post Code	Location of Property Development
Roy	Brown			7 Main Street	Sheffield	0114 219 1234	0114 219 3456	S60 2FF	Puerto Pollensa Mallorca
Marian	Longdale	Cottons Spa Limited	1 Chaffinch Road		Leeds	0845 8900 7812	090 8900 7813	L1 2DF	Alcudia Mallorca Spain
John	Bell	Knutsford Bridge Hotel	Macclesfield Lane		Lincoln	0845 657731	01556 78921	L6 9BV	Mondello Sicily Italy
Roger	Clarke	Northern Bell Company	Azric Drive		Bristol	01454 12234	01454 22564	BS32 1JK	Marbella Spain
Lucy	McDonald	Ullswater Lodge	11 Ullswater Lane		Penrith	Cumbria 01768 1234	01768 2345	CA11 9OJ	Seville Spain

Figure 59

17. In the **F**ield Name, Venue Location, enter a different location for each person in the Address List
18. In the **F**ield Name Date of Seminar, enter a date
19. Click [Close], the Save address list dialog appears
20. Save as Property Development Address List

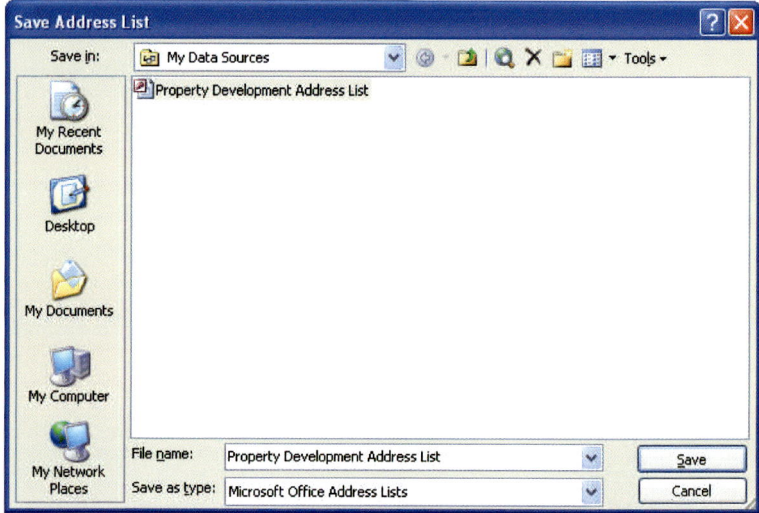

Figure 60

21. Click [Save], the Mail Merge Recipients dialog check list appears

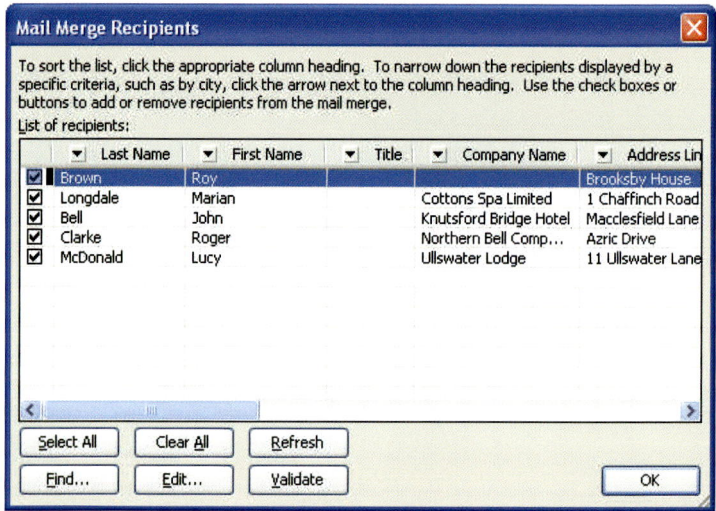

Figure 61

22. This will enable information to be checked and edited
23. Select `OK`, click on Next: Write your letter Step 4

Figure 62

24. Type out the letter below

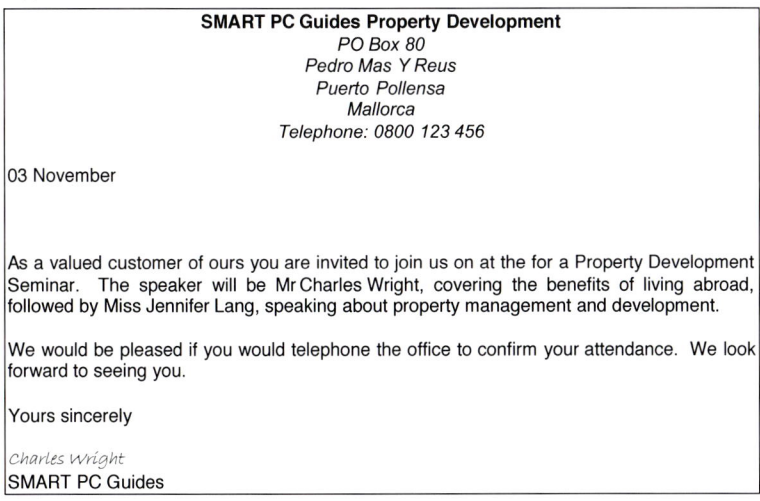

Figure 63

25. Position the cursor where the address is to appear

26. Click on Address Block, the Insert Address dialog box appears

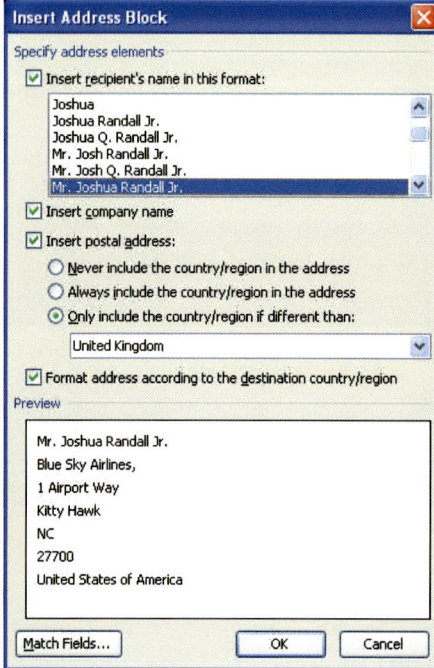

Figure 64

27. Select the required options, click [OK]
28. Position the cursor where the greeting line is to be placed
29. Select [Greeting line...]
30. The Greeting Line dialog box appears

Figure 65

31. Select the required options, click [OK]
32. Place the cursor on the first line of the letter between the words **on** and **at**
33. Select [More items...], choose Date of Seminar
34. Click [Insert], press [Close]
35. Position the cursor between the words **the** and **for**
36. Select [More items...], select Venue Location
37. Click [Insert], press [Close]
38. Choose Next: Preview your letters Step 5

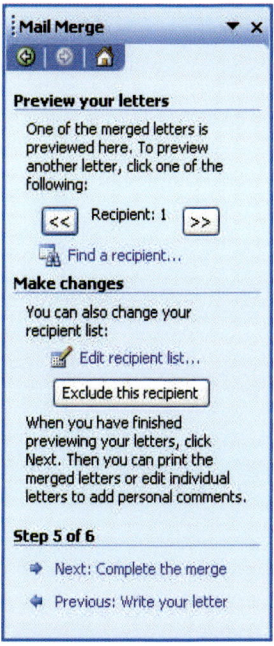

Figure 66

39. Step 5 enables you to preview and edit the final documents
40. Select Next: Complete the Merge Step 6

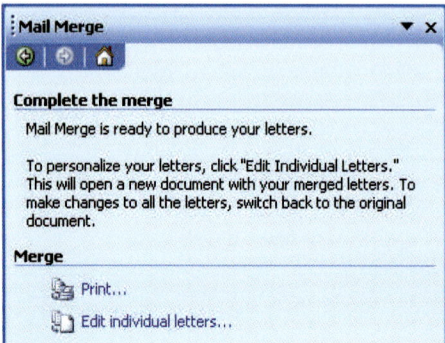

Figure 67

41. Select Edit individual letters

Figure 68

42. The Merge to Printer dialog box appears
43. Select **A**ll, click [OK], the merged document appears on screen
44. Select **F**ile, Print Pre**v**iew, the individual letters can be viewed
45. Select **F**ile, **P**rint, the Print dialog box appears, select [OK]

Creating Labels using Mail Merge

1. Open a new blank document, select **T**ools, [Letters and Mailings ▶]
2. Choose **M**ail Merge, select Labels

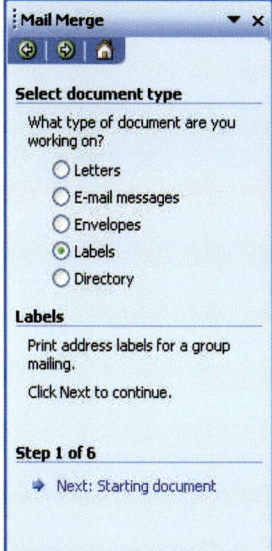

Figure 69

3. Select Next: Starting document Step 2
4. Select Change document layout, click [Label options...]

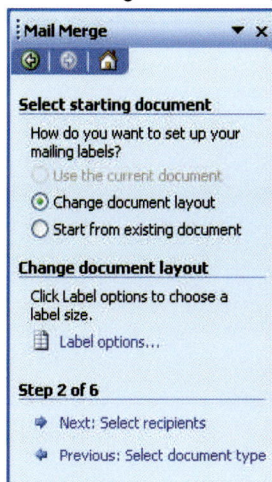

Figure 70

5. The Labels Options dialog box appears
6. Select the required style of your labels
7. Choose Avery Standard 3261L - Label

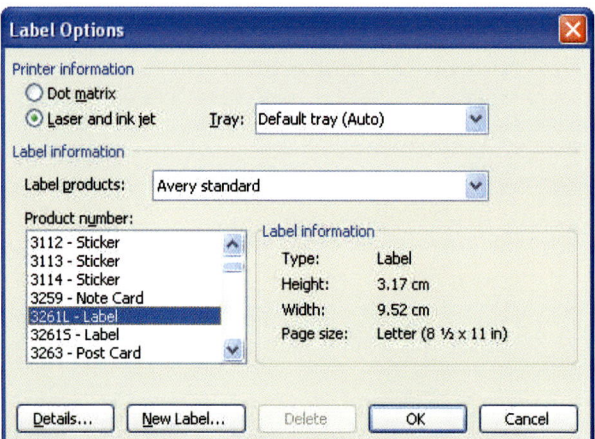

Figure 71

8. Click Details... to display more information on the label

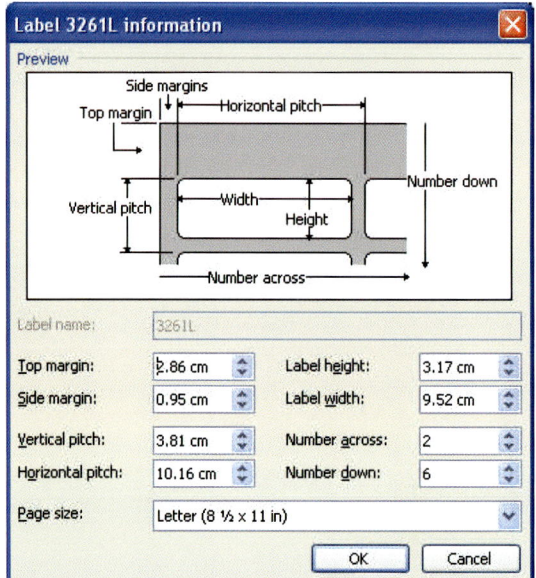

Figure 72

9. Click 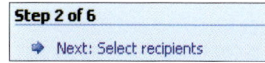 to return to the Label Options screen
10. Press 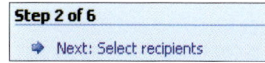 to return to the Mail Merge

Figure 73

11. Select Next: Select recipients Step 3

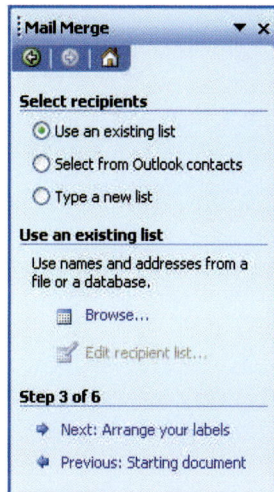

Figure 74

12. Click ⊙ Use an existing list, Select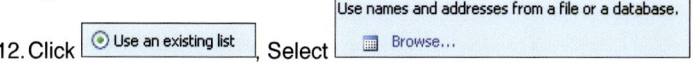
13. Choose the file "Property Development Address List", press [Open]

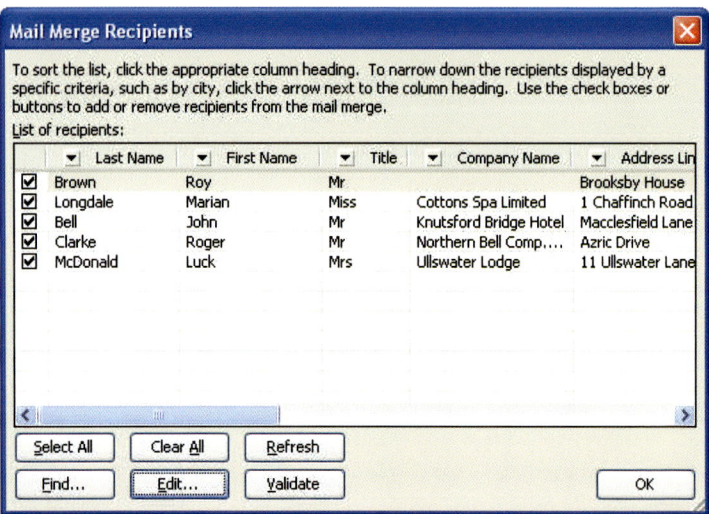

Figure 75

14. Deselect any blank lines by removing the ☑ with the left 🖱 button

15. Press [OK]

16. Click [➪ Next: Arrange your labels]

17. Select [🖃 Address block...]

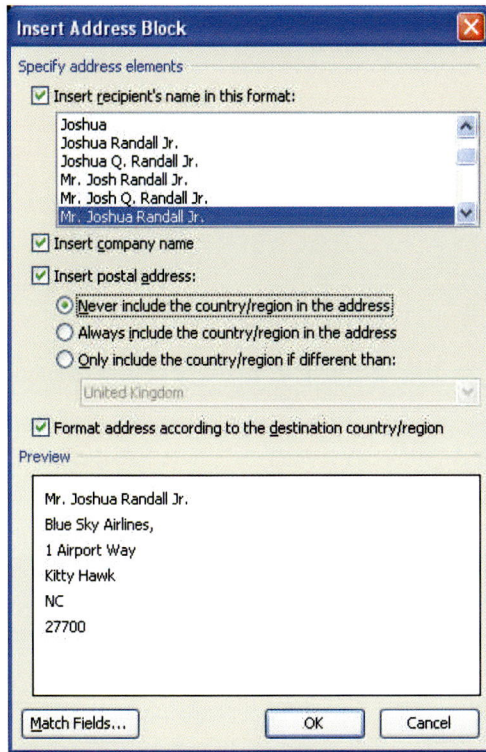

Figure 76

18. The Preview area displays the layout of your label
19. Choose OK
20. The flashing cursor appears In the First Label Box
21. Select Update all labels

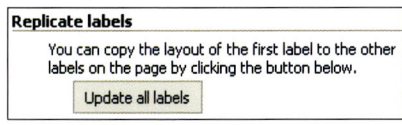

Figure 77

22. Select Next: Preview your letters

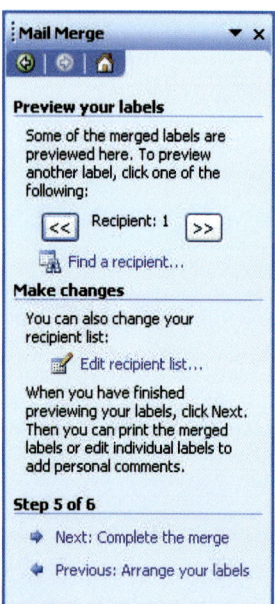

Figure 78

23. Choose ![Next: Complete the merge]

Figure 79

24. Choose ![Print...] to merge the labels

Exercise 6: - Creating Labels

1. Select Tools, Letters and Mailings, Choose Envelopes and Labels
2. Create a labels address for your organisation
3. Select the label style Avery Labels style 3 x 6
4. Reproduce the labels so they appear all on one page in a new document
5. Preview the results
6. Save the document as Company Labels.doc

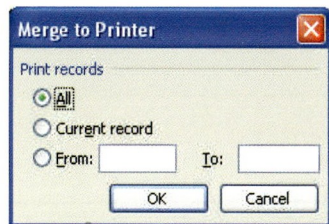

Figure 80

25. Select the appropriate print records option
26. Click **OK** to print the labels